IN OUR SI

Poetry by members of Maryhill Integration Network
Published to mark International Women's Day 2022

Creative Team:

Katherine Mackinnon - Facilitator and Editor

Remzije Zeka Sherifi, Rose Filippi and Anastasia Maria Tariq - Maryhill Integration Network

Sara Abdelnasser - Illustrator

Garry Mac - Designer

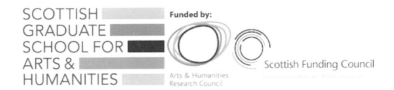

SCOTTISH GRADUATE SCHOOL FOR ARTS & HUMANITIES

Funded by:

Arts & Humanities Research Council

Scottish Funding Council

CONTENTS

INTRODUCTION AND ACKNOWLEDGEMENTS

The book in your hands collects the work of women writers based at Maryhill Integration Network. This is an international collection: different languages float beneath the English lines in these poems, the singing rhythms of Gujarati or a flash of Albanian in a sharp metaphor. Cross-language and cross-cultural, many of the poems were written in group creative writing sessions in Spring 2021. These online writing workshops formed part of my PhD research into refugee and asylum seekers' experiences of everyday life in Scotland, and used poetry by other writers to spark discussion and inspire new poems. Other collective pieces were written for celebrations like International Women's Day, or as part of Maryhill Integration Network's ongoing collaboration with Open Book to provide a space for women to read and write poetry as a means of creative self-expression. Also included are generous, incisive, heartfelt poems by individual writers which express the emotion of the "soul feeling something", as Bisilda H puts it.

Maryhill Integration Network has long been a haven for those of us who love poetry, whether it be writing, reading or listening to the sounds of words. In building such a warm and supportive atmosphere for women to express themselves and to experiment with different creative practices, the staff and volunteers at Maryhill Integration Network have created a treasured space for the unique voices on the pages that follow.

I would like to acknowledge and thank Open Book, who organise and run shared reading and creative writing sessions across Scotland, and whose partnership with Maryhill Integration Network has given so many women the space to read, write and enjoy poetry. I'm delighted to be able to include some poems in this volume which were written in the Open Book online sessions during 2020. I would also like to gratefully acknowledge the support of the Scottish Graduate School for the Arts and Humanities who fund my doctoral research at the University of Glasgow.

Above all, my most heartfelt thanks go to everyone who has participated in the creative writing workshops at Maryhill Integration Network, to those whose voices ring out loud and also to those who listen with intent to the words of others. It has been a delight to work with Maryhill Integration Network and the women of the Oasis Women's Group on creative writing projects over the past five years, and to see a small collection of that work in print is something really special. Most of these poems were written during periods of lockdown in 2020-21, periods which were very difficult for so many of us. Being able to meet up online with these women to read, talk, laugh and write was a light in a dark time. In this book haunting memories of the past interweave through the strong voices of these beautiful writers as they hold forth on the delights, frustrations and dreams of the everyday. Long may they write, and long may we read and listen.

Katherine Mackinnon

CONTENT WARNINGS

These poems present the full spectrum of human experience and contain language that some readers could find triggering, including:

Descriptions of war and sexual violence:

In Our Shoes

Across The Sea

I Want you to know

Descriptions of poverty caused by the asylum system:

Story of a Mother

HISTORY

Group poem March 2021

is in the recipes of our parents.

History is a woman standing in a museum

looking at "The Last of The Clan"

resonating with her own exodus,

leaving everything behind.

History is seeing your own history in the museum of another place

realising history's truths. Entering a room

seeing connections between life in her country

and life in this country:

tools, plates from one hundred years before

still in use. A memory of fresh sheets in childhood.

In the graveyards where people are sleeping

beneath the trees' wide branches,

her hand rests on the stones in silence.

History is leaves pressed in a book.

History is in the wrinkles of a face,

of the mountains. We have always been travellers,

wanderers, on pilgrimages.

History is grandmother's unspeakable stories,

jewels made of steel.

IN OUR SHOES

Remzije Zeka Sherifi

You have never spent days and nights in a cold concrete shelter,

Without water, and electricity…

You have never seen your children exhausted, thirsty and hungry, shaking, asking for just a drop of water or a breadcrumb

You have never seen your dream house grenaded and then blown away in the fire.

You have never smelled smoke mixed with the smell of gunpowder, mixed with the smell of blood…

You have never been forced to watch your loved ones executed in front of your eyes,

You have never been gang-raped, murdered without death,

You have never buried your dreams…

You have never been a political prisoner, tortured and beaten to death

You have never witnessed the most unspeakable stories, the stories of genocide and mass killings

You have never experienced the horror of war.

You have never taken the journey of death, journeys of sorrow and pain travelling the roads through blood pools and across minefields…

Home Secretary, you have never walked in our shoes, been denied seeking sanctuary, seeking the right to work or having a roof over your head...

You have never been destitute, detained, or deported …

RAIN

Anon

Rain, beating against the window...

Echoing the sounds of a young child's heart, pounding with fear...

You imprison me, in this irony of a home sweet home,

Lost innocence, unspeakable truths,

my voice is entombed...

only I can hear you speak, only I know your pain...

A shadowy cloud is looming

and there is nowhere to hide.

ACROSS THE SEA

Remzije Zeka Sherifi

Across the sea

across the hills

far away in my homeland

I witnessed the horror of war

dehumanisation, degradation,

I witnessed murder without death

daughters gang-raped

in front of their parents

wives in front of their husbands

nieces in front of their uncles

mothers in front of their children.

It was an act of killing

but they did not die.

They snatched their innocence,

their dreams, their hope.

What these eyes have seen

what these ears have heard

I wish I was blind

I wish I was deaf

I wish I was dead.

AN EMPTY MAN

Rosa Gracia González

This is an empty man

At home left all

What already lost was

This is an empty glass

As fragile as

Memories of past

We can't understand

The life of a man

Because he is not us

He is the last

our lives go fast

He is just a man

THE FINEST TAILOR

Group poem May 2021

We are still here. Trying to inherit the memories of our children.

Our bond was Friday nights, fish suppers

(although I couldn't afford it every week

so I fried fish in the house, ate it out of newspapers)

my children still carry the taste on their tongues.

My son rings the intercom and I see myself

in the eyes of my mother.

Slivers of ripe conference pears, delight,

cut and shared as a slippery treat.

one a.m. confidences in the quiet kitchen - in those moments

we can really talk, the way we would like to.

Summer vacations, a house with a grandmother

teaching me the handicrafts to keep a house.

The finest tailor made my clothes in the night

while I slept

she cut her sari to make my dress.

Made me gloves to keep me warm,

now I look after her. Every bud and flower in my vase

throws me back in time to the garden of childhood,

full of purest love, my mother's heart.

I miss her touch, and the scent of her skin.

Time with your mother is never enough.

THE POWER

They told you girls don't need education.

Remember your place, obey all the rules.

Listen to your husband and your father

when they tell you:

we own you.

You need to be a lady,

the lines must not be crossed.

You are not our equal.

You didn't listen, refused to give up.

Stood alone in front of powerful men.

You fought for the vote, for the right

to learn and be safe, to love and to work.

You rebelled!

Refused to conform

went on hunger strike, sat down on the bus

with banners raised high you paraded the streets.

The fruits of your labour are delicious today.

Your work in the slums, your beautiful buildings,

the schoolgirls who read books in the sunlight.

Though you are not here,

your words ring out strong

through us your power lives on.

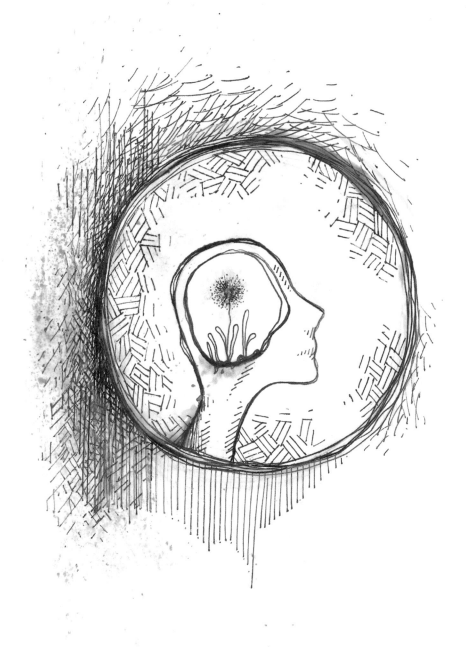

I WANT YOU TO KNOW

I want you to know

that I can't go back. That nobody understands this.

That nobody asks about violence.

Nobody asks about no respect.

Taking the decision to leave, leaving everything you created,

seeing your entire life gone in a second.

I dreamt of seeing snow when I was young.

Standing in a bus stop, someone behind me says

look at her. Look how she's dressed.

They get everything for free.

I want you to know I left all that I had built. I want to work —

why are you stopping me?

I have the skills.

No matter my high qualifications,

my right to work is taken away.

I would have loved to be in my country

where my family and friends are. I was not given

a choice. I was unprotected, persecuted, a victim

of ethnic cleansing, rape, extreme methods

used as a weapon.

"Wouldn't you think about going back where you came from?"

I ask, what do you mean by that?

But I know what they mean.

I want you to know that I had to start all over again.

I talk to anyone in broken English. I am not afraid.

I want you to know that my voice matters,

that I performed on the stage,

dancing like a bird, crossing the earth

with no need of passports or permission.

MY DREAM

Minaxi Champaneri

Back in India, I dreamt of snow

While watching the movie "Evening in Paris"

I dreamt of warm coat, big boots, hats and gloves,

To feel the snow.

I migrated to marry my love in the U.K

He came to pick me up at the airport,

We stopped halfway to the service station for a break.

He ordered the tea and something to eat, I had no clue.

It was a culture and language shock to me,

All through the journey to my new home.

Tea came in a teapot, milk in a jug and something white square in a bowl.

He made my tea and put in that white stoney square.

That white square looked like a marble square we played with back home.

It was a game played by friends with five marble stone squares.

I daren't ask him, why put the marble stone square in my tea?

Those days, sugar cubes were served with tea, I came to know in later life.

I have adapted to numerous things, built our relationship and the family.

I took the cold weather blues, with a light heart,

To support and smoothen up the relation with a flow.

THIS DAY

What would it have been like? Without these people reaching out.

The alarm wakes me / slept through the snooze / rain wakes me / it's dull / and my day is dull / late cup of tea / noises outside / the washing machine / breaks down / the neighbours' washing machine / breaks down / forgot to buy bread / forgot my wallet / slipped on ice / through the door / a letter of refusal / everything starts again / no power to leave / when it rains / can't go out / locked out / anxious / clouded / handed extra at work / without pay / my child is unsettled / cries / the loss of my father / far away.

But this day, a stranger says good morning.

The bread has risen and smells heavenly. I hear music in my language

and there are crocuses in my garden.

Music from my homeland takes me back in time:

a women's freedom song; a story before sleeping.

A friend helps me, keeping us connected.

The window is open   a prayer of thanks.

Scent of lavender and spring blossom, the taste of warm croissants,

children's happy noises, playing in the background.

"Thank you mum! You are the best

in the world." Everyone is pleased with the dinner.

A childhood friend laughs among the sunflowers.

A rainbow fresh in the sky as "Love is in the air"

plays on the radio. I open my eyes

and appreciate the safety I am in. Since I arrived in Glasgow

it's all good days for me.

MY BEING?

Bisilda H

How are you today, me?

after a long sleepless night.

How are you today my body?

that you are keeping me on my feet every day.

How are you today my mind?

that I am not giving you time to rest from my thoughts.

How are you today my soul?

who is enduring so much my pain?

How are you today my heart?

that is beating as if nothing happened.

How are you my half today,

after a part of my soul was detached.

Who is orienting you...?

that I have lost the light of my soul...

DON'T GIVE ME ADVICE

Syeda Sadaf Anwar

You have no idea what it is to walk with hunger.

You have no idea about illnesses without medication,

You have no idea of heatwaves in cold weather.

You have no idea how to tell a toddler there is no milk.

You have no idea about cigarette cravings, somebody smoking.

You have no idea how much you mean to me! I may not be able to touch you.

You have no idea how much respect I deserve! I want,

You have no idea the distance between people! Who love each other,

You have no idea what is struggle with kids, not a piece of cake,

You have no idea how much I sacrifice in migration,

You have no idea how to explain to you!

WALKING IN THE RAIN

Group poem May 2021

Raindrops of window glass, soft smirr of Scottish rain blurring the horizon.

Blurred memories: cloudy sky, the reflection of my sister beside me,

tiny pink and purple wellies, a precious memory. An earthy smell.

Raindrops dancing across our skin in a heavy summer downpour,

the way we used to run outside to feel the rain,

spinning, soaked to the bone, screams of delight. Watering your soul.

In a dress patterned with tiny flowers

I swam in the mud, against the wishes of my mother. Roofs and trees

belonged to my sisters and I.

In a limbo, raindrops sound like a crackling fire.

A couple shelter under one umbrella beside homes,

buildings, windows of hope. I see blossom flying,

passing cars and two girls jumping in puddles,

frocks splashed with mud in this new place.

Acceptance in Scottish society is the sound of rain coming down

on a flat roof, gently drumming.

Raindrops falling in my heart.

Jumping up and down, hair wet,

no need to bring water for the seedlings, green shoots.

I don't mind getting wet if I have a peaceful mindset.

In the reflection of the puddles I see childhood,

the far-off house where I was born. After the rain

the house is in sun, I am with my siblings

surrounded by cherry trees and green hills.

We are walking in the rain, some with bare feet,

some with shoes with holes, making a journey of death

to reach a safe place.

In a puddle I see the colours of this new life.

We walk every day, we are ready to continue the day.

Not waiting for the sun, but waiting for acceptance

waiting for a response. In our shoes we want to walk

under the umbrella of justice. Trying to do the best to survive.

The rain in Scotland has all the colours of an everyday present.

Two little girls jump in puddles,

frocks splashed with mud.

CROSSING THE BARRIERS OF THEM AND US

Group poem April 2021

She loves the taste of this language: proud and real, heartfelt

warm and dry, joyful like a life's song.

A sense of relief after difficult steps.

Everything can be described

across the barriers of them and us. When people greet her

in another language she responds

with a smile. Translating and interpreting,

suddenly faced with the language of doctors

she can do it, can help someone.

Friends mock the pronunciation, say if she'd stayed longer

she would have learned the language.

But she can tell others how she feels, the connection is there.

Languages grow our power. Words bring colour

when we know they will be understood.

When we can open ourselves up to someone, not close the door.

How do you say that in your language?

We're not alone when we have that.

THIS NEW WORLD

Group poem March 2021

I belong where my heart beats. I like to wear animal prints.

My clothes make me stand out. Wearing hijab,

people look at me like I am a foreigner

I belong when I find myself, when I see myself reflected back

kids on bikes shout at us, tell us we are not welcome

I know what that word means.

I belong where I create my home. I belong with my secret thoughts

"one day I will go back", that thought can make me not belong

I belong where I feel safe. I can sing my mother's song

although I cannot be with them in celebration

I belong where the wild geese roost

keeping a distance can keep you safe. a missing community

harms through broken trust

each of us brings a new picture of our country. It is a responsibility

to show what we want to be seen. Every day

brings a person you can learn from

but I need a good night's sleep, without fear

people say "Your accent is not clear"

when I open my mouth. That is not my fault

I accept I am different. I want to survive

In this new world. I need to have friends

good souls

I am human like you.

UNEXPECTED

Bisilda H

Nice sunny day awaiting growing up.

I was living, I thought.

I was imagining and dreaming.

about you, my creature.

Silence prevailed.... the soul was feeling something.

I was afraid to ask but.

I did it because I had no other choice.

What I never wanted and

imagined came suddenly.

What happened? Where was I wrong?

I wanted to accept... it has not been accepted yet.

I heard your heart there along with mine.

Suddenly you were on your way to paradise.

I did not know how to react, but ....

yes, my pain responded with incessant tears.

Suddenly, unaccepted you are gone

I am here crying ....

STORY OF A MOTHER

Syeda Sadaf Anwar

My name is Syeda S. Anwar. I am an asylum seeker in Glasgow since 2019.

I am married and I have two kids.

My son is 9 years old, and my daughter is 4 years old.

The Home Office gives me a very small amount for my family and we can't manage our daily routine life on this small amount. The Home Office does not allow us to work here, as per Government policy.

Me and my husband both are highly educated with working experience back in my country, Pakistan.

We have suffered a lot on a daily basis because the Home Office support is not enough for my family.

As you know that in the UK the weather is so cold and we came from Pakistan and we do not have winter clothes, so we need to buy winter clothes and these clothes are very expensive, especially children's clothes.

My kids demand me to buy toys from shops and we cannot buy from the market because we have a limited amount.

We are belonging to the Muslim religion, and we are using Halal and Asian foods and these foods are not easily available in Glasgow everywhere, we need to go by bus to Asian Store.

For every visit, I have to take a bus ticket. It costs £4.70 for a day pass. It's very expensive for us.

Asylum processes affect my mental health. I feel stress and depression all the time and we do not have any solution to what we do in this condition.

As a mother, I am so much upset about my kids' lives and future in this asylum system.

MY ROOM WITH A VIEW

Oasis Women's Group - Open Book session August 2020

Coloured lights shine down,

shadows on the walls.

Firelight flickering as the wood burns.

The rugs underfoot tell of places I've never been to;

Against a wall sits my grandmother's piano

holding music and photographs.

The view from the window is ever changing

The red, sometimes orange lights on the roofs.

I sit at the window and watch day change to night

and recognise the stars I watched in childhood.

The stars are the same stars.

The room is filled with treasured objects:

the orange mirrored glass jug, shiny and near to my heart

an ancient carving full of traditions that are still part of us

a small clay model on my windowsill casting a long shadow.

The light dims on the room

as the log becomes ash, it falls

leaving pictures in the flames.

A GUIDE TO GLASGOW BUSES

Group poem February 2021

Doors open and close. The bus driver's face

depends on the weather. Be careful you are going

in the right direction, there is no sign.

The bus stop doesn't tell you where you are.

The bus driver and passengers may not welcome you.

They look at you as a stranger, as if you came from another planet.

You might once see the artist, with short white hair

and tattoos on her neck. One day you might see her again.

You might see early workers with laptops out, occupied.

An old man will call you pal, if you take your cat to the vet

everyone loves to speak to it.

Be ready to chat. Keep your ticket. Wear a mask.

It's different languages that are spoken on the bus, slang

banter, jokes. People have arguments sometimes,

talk on the phone. In Glasgow it's always raining.

Babies are crying. Dogs, afraid of being on the bus, shaking.

Remember the importance of coins. You don't get any change.

You might feel uncertainty.

Bus drivers tend to speak really fast. You should know your destination, and the timings.

If you don't click the bell the bus

will

       not

          stop.

If the first floor is full and you have to go upstairs

be careful of the stairs. Say:

thank you driver,

cheers driver,

when you are leaving.

You sometimes need to wait for

the next bus. A lot depends on the driver.

TO MY FRIEND

Group poem written for International Womens' Day

My friend, once we did not know each other.

We started small at first:

a good conversation, gifts for a new home.

We shared a meal, passed the salt

over a table filled with food and teacups, wineglasses

and jasmine flowers.

We went out together,

shared children and responsibilities.

Sister, I chose you,

the family of you and me.

You are honest even if it hurts,

if I need to hear it.

You welcome me in,

unhurried smile and scent of lavender and roses

You make me strong and sing my praises.

My friend, the future is an open door

we go through arm in arm.

YOU GIVE ME

Minaxi Champaneri

You gave me hope

When I sent you my lipstick mark.

You bring me sunshine,

When I only see rain.

You bring me laughter,

When I only feel pain.

You always know,

When to say and what to say.

You give me enjoyment,

When you take me to sunny Spain.

You make my day,

When you just talk to me.

You make me feel I can go on forever,

When you hold my hand.

THE TABLE

Group poem, inspired by The Table by Joy Harjo

Welcome. This table is long

and many people can fit round it.

There is something for everyone, something for all tastes.

I have made for you: bigos rich with allspice and bay leaves.

Salmon baked with rings of lemon.

The table is filled with big platters, chicken baked with yoghurt,

green herbs in the centre, among flowers and candles, bowls of soup.

Vegetables sit on beautiful plates.

My table looks like a market, all the colours are there.

The coolness of raita with cumin seeds refreshes,

with fresh baked bread, many kinds of salads.

Every table is mixed now, with pieces of each culture.

I grew these herbs, dried them, preserved them

for this meal. A jar of rose petal water stands on the table.

My table is me

my culture and tradition, my love and care.

My doors are open for everyone and my salad is famous.

A whole fish wears green leaves, tomatoes and lemons.

It depends on the mood and it depends

on the weather. If it's rainy I must make pakora.

I take a plate to the neighbour.

A THOUSAND WINDOWS AND A THOUSAND DOORS.

Bisilda H, inspired by Refugee Blues by W.H Auden

None of them were ours, my dear, none of them were ours.

Those lights from those windows gave me hope that there is life and

we can illuminate our indefinite refuge.

But suddenly one of those windows would become,

our shelter and every day we will drink our coffee,

and looking out of that window we would think about our future.

In that window every day we saw a little light and

hope that we were being accepted in this community.

We do not take anyone out of this house,

but I am filled with the voices of children and with care as human beings know.

These windows do not tell us whether the residents sheltered there have passports or
not.

We do not depend on a piece of paper like the passport or the words it says inside.

We are the same with the right to be accepted in this community or not because,

our passport does not speak for us, does not work for us, does not think and reason
for us,

does not educate to be worthy in this community but all these we do without these
letters.

We changed some doors and windows but, again we are the same

 who are trying with all the forces of body, mind, soul

and to remain strong invincible.

AT THE LOUISA JORDAN

Mary Kennedy

We join a double snake of neighbours processing through the

aircraft

hangar of a building.

Threads cascade from the ceiling

bearing a suspended labyrinth of metal caging carrying pipes for oxygen to each
partitioned bed

Assorted chairs

An hour from entrance to exit time to contemplate this place its meaning and scale

The kindness of health workers patiently marshalling us towards our shared goal

We felt impelled as walking out we breathed deep the

Clyde's frosted night air and celebrated the rain, our lives,

the meaning of the everyday, while those wards

and cubicles labelled and ranked stood ready.

We walked home grateful.

Our everyday from now, more precious.

PLEASE MAKE A SHADOW FOR ME TO DANCE WITH

Oasis Women's Group - Open Book session December 2020

The eyes of the fox shine their light

while we make a den in the darkness

and tell stories.

An angel is guarding this room -

you might know him as the moon.

An exile returns from fourteen years in the jungle,

sees the light of the village.

Moonlight is very important.

Sparkling, the dazzling glitter of stars,

those rangoli patterns.

Guests come to your home and bring good luck.

To a God we would offer the same:

First some water to refresh.

Small sweets, a plate with many different kinds.

Rice pudding white as the moon

Pistachios, almonds, coconut.

On the top gold leaf sparkles in the dark,

as mysterious as the night

when the first birth of the moon tells us to begin.

WHO IS US?

Minaxi Champaneri

Who is us?

We are human with different colours.

We are human from different nations.

We are all colourful with different fragrance.

We can face many challenges,

We have pride and dignity for ourselves.

We are happy, creative and passionate humans.

We grew up with soil, dirt and poverty with sunrise.

We are human, like others who lives on the earth.

We like to integrate, and rise like sun on the earth.

We like to share our skills to work together.

We hold your hand, and you hold our hands,

To lift us up to share and be joyous together.

This is what, Who is us.

EVERYTHING DEPENDS ON US

Group poem previously published in WWF's Great Scottish Canvas, 2020

The weather in future is important.

Seas without plastic, people each day who care

sowing flowers in every cement back court

to bring happiness and colour.

Can you drink one less juice each day?

Bottles lie everywhere. The protection of rivers and the sky

will make this place colourful and bright.

It is very clear. We need education

for the practical, we need walls made of trees.

We will not cut down a tree to make a house

we will build the house around the tree.

Less concrete

more gardens. Each of us plant a tree

to create this new space. People

will take responsibility for their actions. We can take

from the past, swapping things, growing things.

Rainwater harvesting. Two walkways

along each side of the river. Plenty

of space for us all in this beautiful city. Collect the rain

for the beauty of the garden. A path for our bikes,

no plastic cups, houses which blossom.

Spare spaces can flourish,

walls send messages of respect. Care exists.

We and the animals exist. What we give

is what we get back in return.

CONTRIBUTORS

Anon: I'm a tree hugging, dance-under-the moon hippy at heart. Although I've struggled with depression on and off, I'm always looking for light. As a child when I danced it was the only place I could truly be free. I've found that the arts nurtured my spirit and helped me heal; I wish this for all people.

Bisilda H: I have found the strength through the verses of my poems to express my love, my pain, my feelings to move forward. It is powerful as our feelings speak on paper and remain forever as inspiration.

Mary Kennedy: I'm a wife, mother and Granny. I volunteer with Amma Birth Companions and Woodlands Community Cafe. I sing as often as I can, alone or better still with friends!

Minaxi Champaneri: I am a lover of literature and languages. Writing poems has been my hobby since childhood. My poetry has been published locally as well as internationally in both English and Gujarati.

Remzije Zeka Sherifi: I'm a producer, author, activist & community leader. I believe that creative writing, and other forms of art, are a powerful way to reach out and change attitudes, and that this change propels life for the better.

Rosa Gracia González: I'm a lover of people, communities, and the expression of art through their life's experiences.

Sara Abdelnasser (Illustrator): I believe that life is full of black and white, pain and drama, but from the heart of pain comes out of our head hope in the colour of the sunrise and brings out new life with ideas that are understanding, mature and shining like flowers.

Syeda Sadaf Anwar: Everyone who steps into your life comes for a reason. This project was meaningful for me, I learnt a lot from it through the lovely people. It's my new life, I was born again with my writing skills. My birth place is MIN, as a poet.